Discover Who You Are

The Journey You Have Been Waiting For

Smitha Jagadish

For more information, email:
theschoolforenlightenment@gmail.com

Print ISBN: 978-1-9169074-2-3
Ebook ISBN: 978-1-9169074-3-0

Dedication

This book is dedicated to spiritual seekers looking to discover themselves! Now is your time to move past your struggles and start your journey of self-discovery. This book provides a step-by-step guide, helping you create a clear path to discovering your unlimited potential.

GET YOUR FREE GIFT!

Readers who download and learn from the book
Spiritual Enlightenment
will experience the best results with this book,
Discover Who You Are.

Reading the previous book will help you implement
the ideas in this book more quickly and effectively.
Receive your free copy by sending an email to:
theschoolforenlightenment@gmail.com.

In the subject line, enter the phrase **Free Book**.

Contents

Introduction

Congratulations on purchasing this book. You have been waiting to discover yourself. Now is the time. Step into your spiritual journey and discover your unlimited potential.

You are about to embark on a journey of self-discovery, and this practical book will guide and support you every step of the way as you discover key areas of spirituality. It will also help you understand your different levels of being and the energies within you.

Additionally, this book will help you manage your energy effectively and teach you practices to help you reduce the strain and stress of everyday life.

As you work with the information shared in this book, you will advance your self-discovery journey. Use this resource to answer deep questions that may arise and fine-tune various self-awareness techniques.

Use this to support you and create continuity in your spiritual development. Let it be your daily guide and mentor as you walk the path of discovering who you are.

Part 1:

Discovery

Chapter 1:

Discover Who You Are

Are you ready to connect with your body, unfetter your mind, open your heart, and embrace life fully? Are you ready to explore, learn about, and understand what is happening within and outside you? Through self-discovery, you can live the life you're meant to live.

This book will help you explore the essence of yourself. It will help you learn how to release expectations and assumptions and learn to look within, discovering what makes you uniquely you. Explore your essence. Explore what makes you special.

Society has trained us to identify ourselves, then stop and assume this is who we are. We're taught to live starting from that point. But we must explore further. We must keep discovering and staying open. This book teaches you how.

If I ask anybody who they are, they will say I am so and so: I'm a teacher; I'm a mother; I'm an engineer; I'm a pilot, and so on. But these are worldly labels designed to identify and categorise others easily.

Unfortunately, this identification is often the only way people see themselves; they limit themselves and feel they *are* in a certain box or a category. They're no longer individuals outside their profession or societal label.

Initially, you may temporarily take on this identity lightly, but eventually, you may believe this is all you are. Many people live their entire lives as these labels. We grow within these labels and even develop a sense of belonging to these communities.

We think we *are* teachers, doctors, and workers. In this way, we almost become that identity and never think to or take the time to discover who we truly are.

Every day, you wake up putting on the hat society offers, thinking this is who you are, and you try to be satisfied with it.

These identities have been defined for generations. People know them and are comfortable with them. We're taught from childhood to find an identity box and stick with it. We become consumed with living up to the label—being our best within it—and never think to explore that we're more.

How This Book Helps You Grow

This book helps you discover that you are more than a label. It helps you dive deeper and allows you to chip away at labels society or you have placed on yourself so you can discover your true potential and who you were born to be.

This book is part of a larger journey of discovering yourself. You have broad access to multiple books, courses, teachers, lecturers, and unlimited information on personal development. Though you may read, learn, and intellectually process new information, you likely aren't connecting with all of it.

This book offers a different approach. It guides you through the process of opening yourself up and discovering the reality of your spiritual essence.

This book arises from personal experiences in my quest for deepening spirituality. I'll take you through my spiritual development journey, where I discovered the many parts of me: my physical form, managing my thoughts, how to express love, how to live life, opening to the light of spirituality, and connecting to unlimited potential. That process helped me discover who I truly am. By sharing my journey with you and encouraging you to walk through similar steps yourself, you, too, will discover who you are.

Ultimately, discovering yourself is up to you. No one can do that work for you. Explore the pathway expressed in this book, and you can fully discover yourself and then step into your true potential.

The Self-Discovery Journey

Why do you have to discover your true self? Because if you don't, you may get caught up and stuck in identities that don't reflect your highest purpose. You fall into roles without being aware of who you are. And if you remain in these roles for a long time, you may forget you're meant for something deeper.

Rarely does anyone grow up without being influenced by the outside world. External factors constantly point to you, saying, "This is who you are. This is what you like. These are the characteristics you have and how you should behave." Other people define or label you and mould you into being something, and you don't have the opportunity to discover who you truly are.

Self-discovery is a journey—a beautiful journey where you are in the driving seat. You are the person who gets to uncover who you are. It helps you step away from everything others tell you is true of you. On this self-discovery journey, you'll start exploring your true self from the inside out. You'll realise and bring that essence of who you are meant to be out into the world and live it.

Through this book, you'll learn and implement observation and questioning practices, leading you to discover who you are meant to be.

Benefits of Discovering Who You Are

You might say you're already happy and content, living a satisfactory life. You may not feel a need to find out who you are beyond the life you currently live.

But this current contentment might be temporary. Perhaps deep down, you're not completely settled in your being. As yet, you don't know the true essence of yourself. You've superficially accepted that the life you live is all there is.

You think to yourself, *How I live life is exactly the same way everyone else does it. Why do I need to dig any deeper?*

The benefits of uncovering and discovering who you are—stepping out of the same old familiar routine—are expanded freedom, abundance, peace, stability, and consistency. You're no longer drawn into the external energies or drama around you that are a constant drain. You no longer depend on others to give you the love you crave or the affection you need and want. You fill your own cup.

By discovering who you are, you're peaceful. You're in harmony. You're relaxed. You're stable. You're helpful, and you're open to opportunities when they arise.

Through the years, I've intentionally practiced self-discovery and ignited this desire in others. The people I've coached tell me their journey of self-discovery is something they never even knew existed. Through the training offered in this book and through The School for Enlightenment, they've found an unexpectedly beautiful way to live our life.

7

Knowing who you are from within your own skin rather than continuously looking for answers outside yourself or being dependent on someone else helps you become content and peaceful with whatever you have. You enjoy a fulfilled and joyful life.

I'm living proof of this. I have lived a peaceful and harmonious life for years, and when this peace is disturbed, I know how to return to equilibrium quickly.

I promise you that your life will be enriched by self-discovery. You'll be more open, peaceful, relaxed, and harmonious in your everyday life and feel less stressed, agitated, anxious, and depressed.

Disadvantages of Delaying Self-Discovery

Sometimes it seems scary or like too much effort to set out on a journey to discover who you are. But waiting to embark on this adventure is a mistake.

You might think, *Oh, I don't have time to discover who I am. I'm so busy. I've got children. I've got work. I've got my social life. And what benefit will this add to my life at this point? I'm still young, and I want to have fun. I'm too busy in my middle life with family and friends and work. I'm too old, and self-discovery won't affect the rest of my life.*

But regardless of your age and who you are, waiting to put off personal growth and self-discovery leads to a lack of self-knowledge. Knowing who you are, is the most important thing in life. If you don't do the work, you miss discovering the joy of living in harmony with yourself, knowing yourself, being yourself, and being in the skin you were born to be in.

If you delay self-discovery, you're living your life as someone else or something else. You're focused on goals and achievements designed by someone else.

Discovering who you are meant to be and being that person is the most valuable thing you can do in this lifetime.

It's time to get started. This book can help you. You'll learn about the layers of self-discovery and how to become your most beautiful and authentic self. This book is in your hands for a reason.

Start your journey right now before it is too late. Don't look back and see that you haven't lived the life you were meant to live and been the person you were meant to be. Living the life you were designed for is your most important job. Discovering who you are—even though it takes effort, courage, and diligence—helps you arrive at the life you become your best and destined self.

If you like more support, visit this web address, bit.ly/3Y21sEL, which takes you to the *Discover Who You Are* online course.

Chapter 2:

Spiritual Coaching

Who are spiritual coaches or spiritual teachers? They're people passionate about the world of spirituality who use their spiritual connection to discover who they are and then share their spirit with others.

Often they began their journey at a young age. Many struggled on their own, trying to learn, explore, and stick with spiritual and self-discovery even when it wasn't easy. They had the motivation to persevere through pain and effort, trusting it would lead to greater intelligence. Through constant exploration, they found their way and finally discovered their true selves.

Spiritual coaches or spiritual teachers desire to help others who like to walk the path of spirituality and self-discovery. They help make this path clearer, easier, and simpler. They are inspired to help and guide others, supporting them as they discover themselves, who they are born to be, and their unlimited potential.

I'm a spiritual coach. Since childhood, I've questioned who I was and my life's purpose. Though curious about this as a child, in my twenties, I became deeply passionate about finding the answers. Through a diligent soul-searching process, I began to remove the layers of everything I was taught and told. Slowly, I began to discover who I was. After twenty-five years of consistent searching, learning, and practicing, I've arrived at who I am. I am a new being, free from living up to the expectations of others. My purpose is to support and help you in your journey to discovering who you are.

The School for Enlightenment

Soon after my experience of enlightenment and freeing myself from the identification of the world and by experiencing liberation, I created The School for Enlightenment. Its mission is to help everyone experience enlightenment and guide them to internal peace.

Through teaching an effective and easy-to-follow step-by-step process, the school aims to help you discover your true self and help you reach a state of internal peace.

If you have been searching for who you are, looking to find a deeper meaning to life, or have even been struggling to live an ordinary life due to the pressures of the modern world, the school is here to help you learn simple and effective practices to gain more insight into your life. These practices are Power Flow, Empty Through Living, The Essence of Questioning, Observing the Truth, and Mirror of Consciousness.

These techniques help you to heal and live your life fully by deconditioning, unloading, and freeing yourself from any desires, attachments, and identifications you may have. Through these skills, you can enhance and empower your way of living by gaining pure energy, clarity, and creativity.

The school assists you in the mastery of these practices to become enlightened and to transform into a new being. You will learn to differentiate between truth and falsity, reality and fantasy, violence and peace and start to live a real life of contentment.

The School for Enlightenment shares true experiences. These teachings contain higher energies and experiential truths. The practices have been developed through personal experiences, which have worked for me and many others. I offer all this to help anyone interested in personal development and freeing their consciousness.

The School for Enlightenment also teaches the language of the new being. This language embodies peace, love, and harmony. As more people practice self-discovery leading to spiritual enlightenment, this language will be used worldwide. By learning this language, we will bring forth a world of peace.

This is a new way of communicating with each other and living our lives. It moves us away from the past, which has often taught us to be ignorant of others and ourselves. The school is bringing this language into this world to help everyone find their true self and to experience a new consciousness.

To learn more or join the school, please visit www.theschoolforenlightenment.com.

Chapter 3:

Power Flow Practice

The School for Enlightenment offers two parts to its teachings or practices. The first part is Power Flow Practice, and the second is Self-Discovery Practice.

Power Flow Practice is a meditation where you discover your internal light by becoming aware of yourself in set conditions. You build this meditation over days, months, and years, finally arriving at your highest level of spirituality. This practice helps you cultivate your spiritual life and helps you to heal, rejuvenate, cleanse, and purify so you can wake up energised daily, filled with power, and ready to flow.

The second part of the teachings is self-discovery and Self-Discovery Practice. It is a simple practice that anybody can do anywhere, anytime. It's about practicing detachment—releasing everything we have learned to attach ourselves to.

This practice helps us discover the truth. We begin from where we are. We start at this moment by speaking our truth, by listening, observing, and acting on our truth. The self-discovery practice—founded on truth—leads to the development of intelligence. Once we effectively live in this intelligence, we arrive at being.

These two practices are essential, and they work hand in hand on the journey of discovering who we are.

How I Discovered Power Flow Practice

I moved to England from India in my twenties; I felt empty and had few friends. I searched for anything that would fill that sense of emptiness. It was a new feeling to me, and I had difficulty identifying the words to associate with how I felt.

Someone suggested that I try reading books about spirituality. I had nothing to lose, so I took their advice. Soon I was reading a wide variety of books and watching as many videos as possible. Reading books and watching videos helped me deepen my knowledge, but I still felt unfulfilled and confused, as I did not completely understand what they were trying to convey. This sense of confusion and unclear direction on how to effectively deepen my spiritual life led to disappointment.

I did not know at the time I was searching for my true self.

At that time in England, few people were familiar with spirituality, and I could not find quality teachers I resonated with. I found online meditations that I could practice independently, but the techniques taught were complicated and confusing. Without direct access to a teacher, it was hard to follow anything, and I had no idea where these meditation practices would lead.

Being a wife, mother, and worker, I did not have much time to devote to navigating my mind. However, I knew this learning path was important, and I had to stride ahead. I used to stay up all night, researching, learning, understanding, and experimenting, trying to figure out what spirituality was about.

I could not follow somebody blindly as that was not my way—and that is not spirituality. In spirituality, you are open to experimenting and verifying everything. Whether it's right or wrong for you must be tested on your own, as you cannot simply take someone's word for it. Even though the path was difficult, I was determined to figure it out for myself and see the truth.

Having tried and tested most of the meditation teachings I found online, I still had no luck succeeding at any specific practice. I was distraught and disappointed. I remember going to bed, lying down, and closing my eyes, feeling no hope.

After resting on my back for about ten minutes, something extraordinary happened. I observed that I was slowly relaxing. My body felt as if it was sinking to the ground. The thoughts in my mind slowed down, and my emotions dissolved quickly.

I felt a sense of ease, as though I was out of sync with time. I felt as if I was pulled out of life for a while. It was as if I was totally aware of everything, yet I could experience a deeper part of myself. I felt almost as though nothing from this world could touch me anymore. I felt invincible.

That day, I realised I'd awakened. I was so awake and so energetic that I felt I could deal with anything thrown at me. I was in a state of awe. I had discovered a place of peace and tranquillity. I had found the path to my true self—the inner gates opened. This was the beginning of my self-realisation. My spiritual path had finally appeared, and I was opened to a new way of being.

I discarded all the meditation and other practices that had confused me and decided to pursue my own path to inner peace. Every day I found time to rest on my bed, close my eyes, relax, and stay awake as long as possible. This was a simple, doable, and effective practice.

I would simply lie there and remain relaxed and awake. I started with five minutes, then shifted to ten, and eventually practiced this technique for twenty minutes each day. Finally, over a few months and years, I slowly increased the length of this practice to as long as two hours per day.

After practicing this for about two years, I came to call it Power Flow Practice because this technique gave me immense power to cope with life—to deal with whatever was thrown at me. It helped me navigate life and my mind with groundedness and stability. I now had an enormous amount of strength to face any situation. This practice was a time-out from a busy, hectic, noisy, and overwhelming life. I found an escape route!

During Power Flow Practice, life stopped for me. If you go out for a walk, to the gym, have lunch with friends, watch TV, or read a book, you can relax, but you cannot pause your life. You cannot take a break from it. You cannot sort out the previous accumulations or issues. But through this practice, you create a gap—a gap that helps you come out of this busy life, busy mind, or everyday craziness. It's almost a reset button you can press when you need to recharge yourself.

Benefits of Power Flow Practice

Power Flow Practice helps you completely relax and let go of every tension in your body. Any stress you might have accumulated or any worries over time can be dissolved through this practice. Any longings, emotions, and addictions you might have can all be reduced and eventually eliminated.

Power Flow Practice helps you settle your busy mind and encourages your body to relax. By slowing your mind, you can learn to tap into the unlimited energy available. We all have access to this source of infinite power, which may be dormant and undiscovered.

Power is unconditioned pure energy, the energy that has not been here before and has a quality of newness. This power is potential energy and helps us more clearly see reality.

Power Flow Practice, which anyone can master, is a remarkably simple but effective strategy. You can start at any time, and you don't need any special tools to implement it. The benefits of this practice are life-changing, and the effects are instantaneous.

Through this practice, you'll learn to completely relax and let go of all tension in your body. It helps you ease aches and pains and encourages your body to unwind.

You'll learn to slowly relax your mind. You'll begin to stop your mind and then eventually come out of your mind. This helps you tap into the unlimited energy available to all beings. It helps with creativity, clarity, positivity, high energy, increased mental strength, and better sleep quality.

Regular practice of this technique and learning to access your purest potential energy takes you to levels of accomplishment in life that you never knew existed. You can see the effect of it within three weeks, and you'll move through the phases of awakening, enlightenment, discovering your true self, and finally, liberation. This is a one-stop practice for everything.

Power Flow Practice Technique

Power Flow Practice is best done in a quiet place. A quiet room is helpful as, initially, noisiness can be disruptive. You can also light a candle if it helps you to create a calm and serene environment. You can play calming music to relax and let go of your body.

Lie down and take a break from everything. When you lie down, close your eyes, take a couple of deep breaths, and intentionally stay awake. Don't worry about breathing in any particular way. Focus on the third eye or anything else you may have read about in other practices.

You are completely relaxing. You just allow your body to let go, your mind to slow down, your emotions to be what they are, and your awareness to be free. You have no restrictions, no focus, no concentration. You're being rather than doing.

Start with just five minutes and add a bit more time daily. If you can, try to do this practice each day at the same time and in the same surroundings; it will slowly make it easier for your body and mind to settle into a relaxed and flowing state quickly.

Power Flow Practice Physical Effects

When you lie down and intentionally stay awake, you will notice sensations starting to rise from below. The sensations begin to gather and eventually rise above you.

Everything happens by itself. You don't need to think, label, or understand anything. If you feel like nothing is happening, that's okay. Just stay with the practice of lying still and remaining awake.

You'll slowly notice the sensations in your legs moving upward, and then you'll slowly begin to feel them in your hands, chest, shoulders, and neck until they concentrate near your forehead. This process clears all the tension and stress built up in your body that has moved up into your head.

As you continue with this practice, you'll notice that, eventually, all your body's accumulated tension feels forced into your forehead. If you find this sensation uncomfortable at first, just continue breathing. The discomfort will pass. Eventually, you will sense that this force—this sense of energy—starts to rise above you and move upwards.

When this force rises above your physical body, it's as though somebody's taken away all the tiredness, stress, and tension, bundled it all up, and thrown it above you. The body is relaxed, and you have recovered your body from any strain or tension at this point.

Eventually, you will start to see your thoughts clearly once your bodily sensations have died down. Often, thoughts begin to take the place of physical sensations. You are now entering the mind.

Power Flow Practice Mental and Emotional Effects

Once your bodily sensations fade and you enter the mind, you'll notice your thoughts. They can be short thoughts or long thoughts. They can be old or new. Again, there is no need to do anything. Let the thoughts come and go. You don't need to observe anything. Simply stay awake; that's all that is required.

Often when you enter the mind, you feel you have no direction. No one stands with a signpost saying this is where you need to go, or this is where you need to turn left or right. Free yourself from expectations and allow your instinct to take over. When you were born, you relied on instinct; you learned how to crawl, walk, speak, write, read, and develop intentional thought. It took practice and trial and error.

Taking care of your mind through Power Flow Practice is like learning the art of letting go. By releasing negative feelings and negative thinking, we create space for insights. You exercise your body to stay healthy; this practice is an exercise for your body and mind.

By staying awake, you consciously overcome your body's sensations and disturb the mind's thought patterns. You enter a pure awareness of yourself by simply being without thinking. You are not engaging your bodily, emotional, or mental needs. This practice helps you face your everyday life through expanded awareness. This increased awareness allows you to deal with life situations with clarity, peace, and calm.

This practice also helps you to detach from life's events. Emotional detachment doesn't mean that you no longer care; rather, you can view events from a place of peace and clear-headedness. As you become skilled with this practice, eventually, you'll find that no matter what comes your way, you'll be able to face it calmly and find that solutions arise nearly without effort.

Power Flow Practice helps you reduce confusion in all aspects of life. Where you've been twisted emotionally, you begin to unwind. Solutions to problems become clearer. You start making effective decisions and start seeing life as it is rather than through your veil of emotional or physical responses and temptations. This power you develop is the real power to overcome anything in life.

As you continue this practice daily, you will experience a sense of focused energy in your forehead. As the energy begins to rise from your forehead to above and outside your head, you'll start seeing a light.

Coming into the Light

Initially, this light appears faintly, seemingly at a distance. However, as you practice this meditation—slowly building from five to ten minutes to fifteen and on to twenty and more as the weeks and years progress—you will begin to experience a bright light.

This light arrives after the many thoughts in your mind cease. You'll notice this bright light seems as though it's flowing over you. It clears all your physical pain and all your mental stress. It cleanses you of your built-up emotional struggles and eases your physical pain.

Eventually, with continued practice, you'll float through this bright light, going higher and higher, until you discover your heart has been opened. You begin to connect to yourself and the world through your heart rather than your mind. This bright light becomes a place where you know you can empty your body's tension, where your emotional and mental stresses dissolve, and where your entire system becomes clean and renewed. You will eventually master your breath regulation to an optimum level and tame your life force.

As you clear your accumulated stress and tension over time, you can detach yourself from the unconsciousness that is the old you. You will discover a new consciousness.

Power Flow Practice was the first practice I developed. Over time, it completely liberated me. I hope you will try this practice and that it liberates you as well.

Power Flow Guided Meditation

Power Flow Practice is best done in a quiet place. A quiet room is helpful as, initially, noisiness can be disruptive. Light a candle and play calming music if they enhance your environment. Start with five or ten minutes, and set a timer if it helps you.

Lie down or sit up straight and take a break from everything. Close your eyes, take some deep breaths, and intentionally stay awake. Allow your breathing to flow naturally.

Relax and allow your body to let go, your mind to slow down, your emotions to be what they are, and your awareness to be free. Release any mental restrictions you feel. Release your focus. Release your concentration. You're being rather than doing.

Everything happens by itself, just as it is meant to. You don't need to think, label, or understand anything. If you feel like nothing is happening, that's okay. Just stay with the practice of lying still and remaining awake.

Eventually, you'll notice sensations in your legs—maybe a sense of energy, tingling, or vibration. That sensation starts to flow upward, and you'll feel sensations in your hands, chest, shoulders, and neck until they concentrate near your forehead.

This process clears all the tension and stress in your body. That energy or tension or sensation has moved up into your head. If you find this energy sensation in the forehead uncomfortable, continue breathing; the discomfort will pass.

Eventually, you will sense that this energy force begins to flow outside your body and rise above you.

When this force rises above your physical body, it's as though somebody's taken away all your tiredness, stress, and tension, bundled it all up, and thrown it above you. The body is relaxed. It feels no pain or strain. It becomes free from sensation.

Thoughts now replace physical sensations, and you are entering the mind. You become aware of your thoughts. They can be short or long. They can be old or new. Again, there is no need to do anything. Just let the thoughts come and go; you don't need to observe anything at all. Staying awake is all you need to do.

When entering the mind, you may feel directionless. No one stands with a signpost telling you where you need to go. Free yourself from expectation; allow your intuition to take over.

By staying awake, you consciously overcome your body's sensations and disturb the mind's thought patterns. As you stay awake and practice being without thinking, you enter a pure awareness of yourself.

You are not engaging your bodily, mental, or emotional needs. You begin to face your everyday life through expanded awareness. This increased awareness allows you to deal with life's situations with clarity, peace, and calm.

If emotions arise, observe and detach yourself from them for a while. Emotional detachment doesn't mean you no longer care. Instead, you now view events from a place of peace and clear-headedness. No matter what comes your way, you face it calmly and find solutions arise nearly without effort.

As you continue to remain awake, relaxed, and alert, you notice a sense of focused energy on your forehead. This energy starts to rise above your head, and you see a bright light.

Allow this light to wash over you. It will cleanse you and empty your mind. Remain in this state until you are ready to open your eyes.

Chapter 4:

Self-Discovery

For many years I focused on self-discovery. I wanted to know every bit of myself and attempted to be aware of and understand myself in every possible way. This helped me create a deeper connection with my inner self. Once I learned how to connect with and harmonize with my inner self, all parts of me became unified and formed a new, complete me—a new being.

This process of self-discovery helps you become whole. You connect with all aspects of yourself. You meet your big self, the one that is gracious and kind. You meet your small self, the one that is unaware and asleep. When you bring all aspects of self together and unite them, you become complete. That completeness leads to love. You live in a place of love and express love to others. It creates a beautiful foundation from which to live life.

Self-discovery is a straightforward practice that can be used by anybody, anywhere in the world, at any time. It doesn't follow any rules, patterns, teachings, plans, or complicated training. You don't have to be educated to practice this. It's a very simple way of discovering who you are.

Self-discovery goes hand in hand with Power Flow Practice and helps you discover your being—who you are—the unified you. Self-discovery helps you connect with your physical, mental, and emotional energies and discover your inner light, which helps you deepen your spirituality. Self-discovery helps you find your truth. This powerful combination of self-discovery and Power Flow Practice helps you arrive at your inner self.

Finding the Truth

Self-discovery begins with truth—speaking the truth, seeing the truth, observing the truth, listening to the truth, and acting from the truth.

But initially, we don't know the truth because we live a life filled with lies. We speak lies. We hear lies. We act on lies. Without self-discovery, we don't know the truth. We live in a state of confusion. It's nobody's fault. It's just how modern life has evolved.

It is up to us to begin self-discovery by speaking the truth, seeing the truth, listening to the truth, and acting on the truth. We must choose to live the truth. We cannot begin self-discovery anywhere else. We have to begin from where we are.

When you choose to take conscious truthful action, you promise yourself that moving forward, you'll speak only the truth. You'll choose to hear the truth and act from the truth. This is where the self-discovery begins.

Slowly, day by day, as you practice self-discovery, you build your awareness of truth by observing life. For example, right now, notice what is around you. Just observe your surroundings. What do you see? What do you hear? What do you feel? How are you behaving? What are you thinking?

By observing yourself, right now, in this present moment, you consume the truth of this moment. You absorb the truth that is happening around you. When you see, hear, observe, and connect with what is around you, you can authentically act. Because you've seen, heard, and felt the truth of what is happening in this present moment.

Opening Awareness

Open yourself to awareness. I'm not referring to an intellectual grasp of what is happening in our world, nation, or family. Self-discovery doesn't arise from a cerebral way of thinking.

Instead, open yourself to an awareness of feeling. What are your thoughts—not thoughts of the world but your internal thoughts?

Ask yourself:
- *What am I thinking, and is it the truth or lies?*
- *Where am I in my feeling journey?*
- *Where am I in my actions?*

- *How am I behaving daily—how do I greet and talk with people?*
- *What do I speak—do I speak what I see as the truth, or do I make up things?*
- *Am I funny or a little bit extravagant?*
- *Do I think about myself—my career, my passion?*
- *Or am I thinking about hurting somebody or planning a plot?*
- *Am I lost in my thoughts or daydreaming?*
- *What sort of thoughts do I have?*

This is where you begin. Start in the present moment and explore who you are from right now. Write your thoughts, feelings, and actions in a journal. Even though, at this point, you don't fully know the truth, you're starting to dig the ground.

The self-discovery process is like digging to find water. But we don't know how the water will taste or where it is, but somehow you sense its unlimited potential and have a deep need to find it.

You're in control of your self-discovery journey. You're the one digging for water, leading the way. You have nothing to lose. No one is manipulating you. You're not in danger. No one else can stop your exploration. Only you can stop this journey. Only you can give up and say, "I've had enough." Sometimes the work is challenging, but the end result is worthwhile.

Write your actions, reactions, thoughts, and feelings daily. Good and bad. Then keep digging. Keep digging, and see what you discover each day. Each day, you'll discover something new, something fresh that you have never seen in yourself. You'll discover things that no one else has pointed out to you. You're not relying on somebody else's words or somebody else's perspective of you.

Clearing the Past

Self-discovery is about clearing the past. You're uncovering and recognising *your* authentic words, feelings, and actions. You begin to release the influence of others and begin to connect with the pure you.

This connection to self becomes clearer every day, every minute. You're in self-discovery. You're clearing your past. You're clearing the things others have told you about yourself—things you have not discovered on your own—and freeing yourself from lies of your past. You're detaching from other people's thoughts, feelings, and actions that you once believed defined you.

You're clearing old thoughts and patterns taught by your parents, friends, relatives, teachers, icons, society, and the world. A multitude of people have influenced you growing up. Now is the time to clear that influence.

Clear it with respect by thanking all others for helping you get this far. Know that they've helped you reach a point in life where you acknowledge that you now need to discover yourself. This is a beautiful place to be.

Your journey begins. Slowly and daily clear out the thoughts or influence of others. Learn to differentiate your thoughts from theirs. Learn to differentiate your feelings from somebody else's feelings, your life from somebody else's life. Love yourself as you are without relying on the love of others to make you whole.

Each person must discover himself or herself. You cannot do this for anyone. They can not do it for you. We are individual beings, differentiated from each other. This individual work, this individual awareness helps each of us arrive at our true potential. This process is filled with awe, wonder, beauty, and energy.

Connecting with Intelligence

When you begin thinking new thoughts for yourself—thoughts that originate from within you—they have a different type of energy. It's so powerful that you'll barely be able to contain it. You'll want to jump up and down and shout to the world, "Listen! This is what I've discovered"! The feelings that arise when you discover something are exuberant. This euphoric feeling may last two or three days because you've unlocked internal energy.

Bit by bit, shovel by shovel, you start to discover new thoughts, ideas, and feelings that are solely your own. This newness keeps popping out of you. Every single minute. The more you listen to yourself, connect with yourself, and trust yourself, the more your abundance will flourish.

Take time to write down what you see, hear, and act on every day. Observe yourself and take notes. You may not notice much at first, but slowly and steadily, you'll get the hang of it. Journaling or writing notes and reviewing them will help you see your growth pattern.

You will see how your intelligence grows. Intelligence is what actually connects you to yourself. Once you start with the truth, then you connect it with intelligence. Because the greater truth is intelligence, you become this intelligent being where everything acts by itself. You have cleared out the rubbish and developed your innate truth to a level of ultimate intelligence. Now this intelligence acts by itself in everyday life. It shows you whether what you're doing is acceptable or not. It shows you if your actions are in sync with the universe being that you are.

So, in this way—starting with self-discovery, starting with the truth—you'll arrive at intelligence and begin living a harmonious life. Intelligence is now operating in you. This intelligence is new. You've created it by doing the work of self-discovery. You've become an authentic, unique, intelligent human being.

This intelligent human being starts to live its life now. And this intelligent life will observe everything that is happening at every moment. It can recognise that which suits and which doesn't. It will bring harmony and truth to your life.

You're in sync with everything in and around you. The moment you come across something that this new intelligence within you disagrees with, you'll reject it. And in this way, you will start to live your life every day in intelligence, attracting the things that will grow this intelligence into an even bigger self. When this starts to happen—when this intelligence keeps progressing over the months and years—you will arrive at your core being. This is the true purpose of self-discovery.

Self-discovery is simple and self-reliant. You begin with the truth and cultivate your intelligence to a level where you live as an intelligent human being. You have power over your mind, power over your body, and power over your emotions. You live simply, easily, harmoniously, and truthfully.

Part 2:

Levels of Being

Chapter 5:

Introduction to the Levels of Being

Let's begin with an overview of the levels of being and how they work together. Then we'll explore more information about each level.

The School for Enlightenment introduces levels of being as a way to recognise the different energy types within us. In the graphic on the next page, you'll see a brief description of the many layers of energy that we live in every day.

Our most basic energy is the energy of the body. As you can see, energies ascend from there, leading from the energy of the body to the energy of the mind to love, life, light, and energy synthesis.

Then we move into a new state of being, and above this new being is liberation. Liberation leads to unlimited potential. Details about individual energy layers will be explained in subsequent chapters.

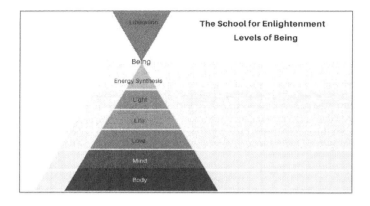

Most of us are familiar with many of these layers. We have experienced them. We have been in them. We've been out of them. We've been caught in them. And now, it is time to recognise them clearly in daily life at the moment we're in them. It is time to notice more clearly how energy levels work.

It is time to contemplate the following questions:

- *How does my body function?*
- *What are the forces that hold me here?*
- *What is the weakness that I have in this energy centre?*
- *What is the weakness that I have in the centre of my mind?*
- *What is the weakness I have in the level of love?*
- *What is working or not working in my life?*
- *Do I feel connected to my light?*

Asking yourself these questions helps you recognise these levels not in theory but as practical learning in your day-to-day life. By recognising which energy is more pronounced in any given moment helps you balance it with the other lacking energies. Understanding this Levels of Being chart helps you sense your energies, work with them, and detach yourself from them if you're feeling stuck.

In the next graphic, we see arrows going downward and upward. The downward arrow represents attachments, and the upward arrow represents letting go.

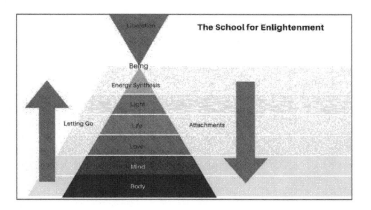

In other words, imagine being in the layer of love, experiencing its beautiful energy. Then unexpectedly, a random disturbing thought pops up, and you immediately disconnect from that feeling of love.

You've dropped into thinking—the level of the mind—and you're now attached to worrying about the disturbing thought. You can see your attachment to thought and worry drop you down a level. When you let go of the thought or worry, you can rise back up.

This chart helps you see how attachment pulls you down into different layers and how letting go of these attachments helps you rise upward. Through conscious awareness and effort, you can move upward through the levels.

As another example, imagine overthinking during the day. If you recognise you do this, you can consciously take a moment to express gratitude, kindness, or love. Sharing joy, caring for somebody, or genuinely smiling at someone will immediately lift your energy, and you'll rise to the level of love.

Through self-awareness and self-discovery, you begin to recognise the various layers and when you move up and down through them. You can choose at any moment to lift yourself upward. As you ascend the layers, you become lighter, feel better, have a positive attitude, and live a simpler life.

The next graphic illustrates the shape of a person representing our being and the energies behind it. Once you learn about and recognise these energy layers within you, you can choose how to implement them to help you feel better throughout the day. You learn that attachments can pull you down and that letting go helps you ascend.

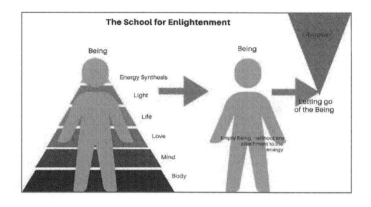

Once you become aware of these energies, work with them, and master them, you attain a level of energy synthesis, the topmost energy level. Energy synthesis is where all the energies come together; you no longer recognise individual energies. This is an exhilarating place to be because, at that point, you have an incredible amount of energy within you working together as a whole. The energies of all the layers are in harmony and synchronous. You're not divided; you're completely whole.

When you arrive at this point of energy synthesis, you attain the state of being. This state helps you live in a place of energy synthesis. When you live in this combined energy—pure energy—you no longer differentiate between any of the other energies.

Your being becomes its pure self, the one who witnesses everything. It has no purpose but is transparent and simply present in every moment. In that state of being, you'll be able to recognise the difference between the being and the energies themselves.

Once you recognise your sense of being and are comfortable there, you'll understand that you've emptied your different energy levels entering into the being, and you're no longer attached to them. You'll come to a point where you no longer need the differentiation of each energy level. You've released attachments and become a unified being. When you spend enough time as the being, you realise its time to let go of the being, too, as it serves no purpose without the energies. When this happens, you become liberated from the energies and the being. You are free. You aren't entangled anymore.

You enter into a void, an emptiness. You are in a new space, and this space opens up to unlimited potential. Unlimited potential leads to the discovery of who you are.

Remember to reach this place of unlimited potential, you follow a sequence of steps.

You're a person with a body—perhaps healthy and fit—and you're aware of your body, but you know life has more to offer than simply connecting with your body. Then it's time for you to move up to the next level, which is the mind.

You enter the mind and take the time you need to explore the level of the layer of the mind. When you're content in the mind, you still like to explore more, so you move into the level of love.

Once you steep yourself in love—for yourself and others—you begin to feel ready to rise again. You move up to the next level, which is life.

At this level, you recognise the joy of living rather than accumulating. Previously we've accumulated material goods, social accolades, jobs and promotions, and love. Accumulation leads to a horizontal journey within a level rather than an upward trajectory.

For example, if you're in the level of love, instead of basing your sense of self and love on more people, more family, more enjoyment for relationships, and more community—all of which is sideways expansion—you could honour what you have and choose to move upward. Moving upward helps you explore life; you begin to feed yourself to find out about, discover, and explore life.

In other words, nothing requires you to stay stuck at a particular level. If you do stay at one level too long, you may get bored, frustrated, and disheartened because you're not learning and growing. Every day becomes the same.

Imagine you're wealthy. You have all the money you need, yet you feel dissatisfied. You're bored and don't know what to do, so you get into trouble. This dissatisfaction arises because you're not ascending to the next level; you're not discovering the next layer that you need to challenge you and keep you growing.

It is essential to observe and then identify which level or layer you're in. See where you're overdoing something or connect with that sensation of stuckness. Then refocus your efforts on detaching from your current routines and put your energy and effort into moving upwards. Travelling horizontally is merely repetition. Ultimately it doesn't take much effort. It's just obsession. If you're obsessed with something or addicted to something, it's because you're going horizontally rather than vertically.

So as you practice self-awareness and self-discovery, and write about it, remember this little hint. *If you are obsessed with something in your life, it's because you're going sideways. Take the energy you use to obsess and use it to move upwards into different levels.* Taking this intelligent action will help your life flourish in satisfying and creative new ways.

If you'd like to learn more about these levels and want personal guidance, go to this website, bit.ly/3Y21sEL, which takes you to the *Discover Who You Are* online course.

The Value of Discipline

It is also worth noting that this process of self-discovery takes discipline. Often the term discipline is misunderstood. Some people view discipline as brutality or punishment, but that is not how to view it in this instance.

On this journey of discovering who you are, you'll explore all your energy levels. It is difficult to manage these energies because they have extreme natures and are all over the place when they are agitated.

This is where discipline comes into play. Discipline gives you the courage, stamina, and support you need as you move to the next level. Self-discovery requires clear-headed and open-hearted observation and tremendous love for yourself.

Consider the term discipline to mean maturity—maturity in oneself, not behaving like a crazy spoiled child. Discipline, in this context, means responsibility. You're responsible, mature, and disciplined enough to observe and understand the depth of your learning.

Discovering who you are is a hard task. Yet it will help you have a balanced life. It will help you reach your true nature.

Chapter 6:

Level 1: The Body

All of us have a body. Having a body is essential to being human. But are you helping your body function optimally? Do you honour your body but not obsess about it?

The goal of this body energy level is to find balance and health. Connecting with your body doesn't mean weighing, measuring, or competing. Instead, learn to connect with the body's innate intelligence.

What Is a Body?

You're familiar with the notion of a body; you have one. At birth, recognition of your body is the first awareness you have. Through the years, you learn about your body. In childhood, adolescence, and in adulthood, you continue to learn about your body. You learn how to look after it, how to strengthen it, how to feed it, how to keep it healthy, and to extend longevity. You invest your time, effort, energy, and money into maintaining your body.

It needs constant attention. It needs cleansing. It needs feeding. It needs nourishment. It needs relaxation. Every day you spend time taking care of it. You maintain a healthy body to combat the fear of losing it, hurting it, or having a problem or disease with it. The process of maintaining your body is endless. You can see the importance of your body and its energy to your life. Think about how much money, time, and emotions are spent shaping this body and maintaining it for its longevity.

Your lesson is to identify the body's energy and recognise how much time you spend on it. Sometimes it becomes easy to obsess over bodies. Perhaps you track everything you do for your body—what you eat, how you exercise, how you digest, how you sleep. Perhaps you research how to take care of your body—you read about disease and how to prevent it or read about the latest fads for diet and exercise. Tracking and research take energy.

Now that you better understand your body, it is time to learn new ideas about how to care for it well and healthfully.

Listening to Your Body

From a young age, you receive messages from sources outside yourself about what an ideal body is or should be. External influences—such as family, friends, school-mates, and co-workers—tell you what is considered to be a good body, a pretty body, or a beautiful body.

You learn what is right and perfect from others, followed up with messages that you need to fit into a particular box with no exceptions. Accepting and reconciling these messages with how you are in reality is often a struggle.

You try to shape the body you're born into with society's ideal norms and expectations. You're in constant conflict, trying to match reality with an imagined ideal. This conflict creates so much tension, pressure, unhappiness, and depression that you may give up and live life unhappily if you perceive you've failed to achieve this ideal. You begin to believe you don't have an ideal body and can never attain it.

Or, perhaps you are ambitious and can ignore other areas in your life to achieve this ideal body. Yet the process of achieving this ideal body causes you to give up everything else you may have innately enjoyed. This ambition does not lead to a satisfying win. You still haven't got it all—to achieve the win, you've given up everything else.

Focusing on getting something you don't have or worrying about not being good enough wastes energy. It's a game you play but often don't know you're playing. Exercising and maintaining good health is critical for longevity. But trying to achieve an ideal body is a waste of time.

Once you let go of this attachment to the ideal body, you start to embrace your body as it is. You realise how it functions and what it needs. Shifting into this awareness requires intelligence. It requires self-awareness—noticing what is natural—rather than using analysis of social norms and expectations to drive results.

Your Body's Innate Intelligence

Use your body's intelligence to tell you what it enjoys, what works for it, and what doesn't. What works for you may not work for someone else. You could be working with a famous physical trainer, and they offer excellent advice. Yet, that advice doesn't work with your body. No matter how hard you try. It doesn't work, and you're not enjoying the process. You realise you need to be your own personal trainer. Transformation might take a long time, but at least you are following your innate intelligence.

Life is all about developing the intelligence of your body, your mind, your heart, and your life and allowing this intelligence to flow through you rather than trying to learn from an outside source. It is about self-learning and self-educating rather than absorbing and assimilating someone else's version of right or wrong. Choosing to acknowledge this allows your intelligence to grow.

With this new perspective, you begin to exercise by first allowing your body to be intelligent. How does this happen? Start by disregarding everything you've been told is the right way to create an ideal body. Simply detach from and forget all that external stimulus. This helps you become free.

You're free from comparing your body to those you see in pictures—you detach yourself from believing you need six-pack abs or an hourglass figure. Once you let go of the attachments, you'll have a clean slate and can begin listening to what your body tells you.

Wake up in the morning, and then simply sit with your body for five or ten minutes. Notice how you feel. What is your body telling you? It might be difficult to identify initially, but be patient and keep trying. In addition to listening to your body, notice what your mind and emotions are saying. Eventually, you will get to know your body, your mind, how you feel love, and how you like to live. It is a process, but one worth exploring.

Listening to Your Body

At this moment, you likely have confused emotions; they all speak different languages. You may hear different messages coming from different places—within you and outside of you. Quietly listening, without expectation, begins to clear the noise and lead to greater self-understanding.

Listening is your greatest tool. Begin to discern the difference between craving and hunger, the difference between sleepiness and exhaustion, and the difference between fatigue and boredom.

Sometimes you feed your body, but in reality, it is tired and needs to rest rather than eat. Sometimes you're fatigued, but rather than resting, you really need to hydrate with water. Or sometimes you know you're hungry but don't give your body the right food. Listening helps you offer yourself the right answers.

As you listen, write down what you hear and notice. Daily identify or distinguish your body's responses. By listening, you become aware. Awareness leads to intelligence. Your body begins telling you what it requires. No longer are you forcing your desire on the body. When this happens, you become freer, less forced, and you have more time on your hands to do something else.

Simply listening and identifying might feel like doing nothing. Yet it is a wonderful tool. You'll be able to recognise pain and discomfort before it becomes severe. You'll be able to recognise tiredness and lack of energy and contrast that with vibrance and balance. When you listen, you'll become aware of your body's intelligence. It knows how to create enough energy to sustain itself. It is not necessary to try too hard, to overwork yourself.

You have all you need. You simply need to become open and aware of it. Bring awareness to the innate intelligence of the body. Free yourself from external attachments and look within. This choice leads to optimal health.

Moving Toward Mind

When you've listened, learned about, and connected with your body, you feel healthy and strong. You honour your physical form and do what is required to take care of it. But you've just started! You have more layers to discover. The next layer is your mind. Though you feel great in your body, it is time to address your thoughts.

Chapter 7:

Level 2: The Mind

The mind is a tool. It helps you think, reason, analyse, remember, and recall various life activities. You learn how to use it as you grow up. From childhood, as you learn to understand your body, you also learn to understand the workings of the mind. You learn how to speak, converse, and interact with people. You learn to read and write. All of these things come from the mind, which is an integral part of human development.

You use your mind almost every hour—nearly every minute—to process all the information coming your way. You are constantly learning, thinking, remembering, recalling, and using your thoughts to do this. Your mind plays a huge role in this day and age with technology. Additionally, mental creations lead to advancements that often help preserve your body. In many cases, jobs now use minds more than bodies.

The development of technology through the use of the mind helps you maintain closer communication with your friends and neighbours locally, nationally, internationally, and globally. Your ability to communicate from one end of the world to another is all due to the development of the mind.

What Disturbs Peace of Mind?

Each brain is different from the next. Each person has his or her own life experiences. Yet, we all have similar experiences of being human, and we all have a mind.

Your life experiences affect your peace of mind. How others speak to or behave toward you affects your peace of mind. If somebody has said bad things about you or has been disrespectful to you, your mind is affected.

It is up to you to care for your mind, reforming it and refining it. It is up to you to practice forgiveness of others and yourself and release painful memories you may cling to. Hanging on to painful memories or the past spoils present-moment peace. A healthy mind likes to forgive and be forgiven. It likes to respect itself and others. It likes to speak freely yet kindly.

Imagine being in love. How do you speak to your loved one? What actions do you show? You may not speak or act kindly if your mind is under stress. In the long run, this meanness causes a crack in the relationship, and peace of mind collapses. Your loved one leaves; you no longer have peace. You're back to square one, where the mind is unhappy and searching again to find love.

Thinking versus Creating

Thinking is different from creating. Thinking is your capacity to manipulate words and actions in your mind. Creating is the act of forming new thoughts and ideas in the present moment—in the now. It is up to you to choose whether you spend more time thinking—which often looks like the truth but may not be—or creating by being in the present moment, presenting fresh, unique ideas to the world. Creativity arises when we're connected to the whole while being aware, alert, and awake.

Your actions and spoken words are the most important thing in the present moment. Nothing else matters because your words and actions in the now represent creation. When you create through actions and words, a memory is formed. As you learn to work with your mind, you strive to create beauty, love, joy, and happiness. Be aware, awake, and alert while you're creating.

Moving Toward Love

But human development doesn't end at the mind; there's more to discover. According to The School for Enlightenment classification of Levels of Being, the next level is love. The jump you need to make now is from mind to love. This leap must happen as quickly as possible because the mind is a great tool for development, but overuse can be detrimental.

For example, technology can help humans lighten the body's load, but it can also extinguish life. Using the mind excessively may destroy the body through stress, anxiety, and other mental illnesses. To prevent destruction, you must move away from obsession, find balance, and shift into the level of love. The act of creation, when done harmoniously, also leads to love.

Chapter 8:

Level 3: Love

Love is the feeling you have towards somebody or something. Feelings can be negative or positive. You have negative feelings when you are attached. When you love a person deeply and become attached, if something happens to that person, it's almost as if you feel their pain. This love you feel could be for an individual, a group, a community, or a nation. You can feel love for anything—a job, your body, or your mind.

You use love to create connection, attraction, closeness, intimacy, and romance. It encompasses an immense energetic layer, a beautiful layer. As with anything, love can have two sides. Sometimes love makes you feel beautiful and ecstatic, like you're flying high. But at the same time, it can also make you feel low, depressed, unhappy, and sad. This volatility arises from our attachments with friends, family, and other loved ones.

Love helps you see beauty. It helps you connect deeply with something or someone, and your energy flows outward. Ideally, your loving energy is reciprocated, flowing back to you. Love can act as a mirror. If you show love towards something, love is reflected back.

Love helps you to share what you have with another person. It teaches you to understand other human beings. It teaches you to understand relationships. It teaches you to understand the feelings that are integral to being human.

Love connects you to family, to growth, and to human expansion. Through love, you create children, which leads to community growth. Love supports creation and enrichment. Once you reach this layer, it feels good to spend time there. It is beautiful and uplifts you. Even when love is painful at times, you still crave it. Again and again, you like to return to it.

Love is different from thinking. It has a different energy than that of the mind.

The Duality of Love

One encompasses spirituality, love, and intelligence. The other encompasses body, money, and work. These two aspects are the opposite of each other—the two sides of the same coin. They're not good or bad. They're not right and wrong. They're simply different from one another, working in different ways. Both are useful. Both are needed. Your responsibility is to find harmony between the two, not competition.

Look for and observe both aspects within yourself. Intelligently honour the value of each, knowing that one is not better than the other. When you can do this, it helps you better appreciate both and leads to a better-balanced life.

However, it is not uncommon to live a life out of balance. You see the world in negatives and positives. When you're out of balance, you constantly search for the opposite of where you are, even if unconsciously. This separation often leads to fear—fear of accepting or loving something you perceive to be the opposite. By consciously harmonizing both aspects of self, you create oneness, and the fear dissipates. In this oneness, you will see who you truly are, and the beauty of life will unfold in front of you.

Love in Relationships

Successful relationships have three elements. For any relationship to grow, you need to balance love with the body and mind. Those elements woven together support a healthy and flourishing life.

But sometimes attraction to another is so profound we forget to stay connected to the body or mind. We attend solely to love and fall out of balance. This lack of balance often results in the death of a relationship. You must integrate body, mind, and love to sustain healthy relationships.

Once you have created a relationship that balances body, mind, and love, you'll experience an uplifting life, and you can take the relationship to the next level. It becomes essential that you and your loved one balance the primary three elements.

In other words, each of you must know yourselves. Each of you must be fulfilled as a person alone. When you come together with another balanced person, and you are in love, each of you begins to more clearly explore this beautiful life together. Day in and day out—in each moment—you are balanced and are no longer lost in your emotions. You have a life of your own as well as the relationship that you willingly share with another.

This approach supports a harmonious relationship. You are aware of yourself and aware of your relationship. You are aware of the other person and aware of the love between you. You are living your life and maintaining a healthy relationship. You are manifesting love and moving toward light. You and your loved one have created something new. It's almost like this relationship has become its own entity.

Love as One

During the years when I focused on self-discovery, I tried to understand myself in every possible way. I heightened my awareness and my place in the world. That introspection and contemplation led me to feel a profound sense of unity within myself.

You can attain this state as well. Your self-discovery leads to a blissful feeling of love, of wholeness. If you haven't yet fully discovered yourself, continue noticing and practicing awareness until you begin to feel whole.

There is always some part of you looking to discover the big self, small self, and all aspects of yourself. Try and look for and find each other until you are complete. Once you're in union with yourself—harmonizing all parts of yourself—you are totality. You embody love. You express love. You live in love, and it is beautiful.

Moving Toward Life

When you're at the level of love, you feel everything is possible. You're at the top of the mountain. It seems everlasting, like it's forever. But remember, you have more layers to discover. The next layer is life. Though love is gorgeous and feels sublime, it is time to leap from love to life.

Chapter 9:

Level 4: Life

When we were born, all we knew of life was our immediate surroundings. We played in the Garden of Eden. We played in this beautiful place of heaven. We lived in paradise, where everything was forever eternal, and we rested in the heart of God.

As years passed and we began to grow up, we became aware of life's duality—woman and man, right and wrong, good and bad. Oneness was split into many, and we learned separation. We learned to label—I'm a girl, you're a boy, you're a woman, you're a man. You're a mother; you're a father. The list of splits goes on.

When this knowledge entered you, you forgot the essence of who you were. You forgot the notion of utopian eternal life. You forgot oneness. As separation continued, you deeply desired to become one again. Throughout your life, along your entire journey, you go through suffering, pain, and worries, searching to become one again.

How do you become one? What is that oneness? What will give you the feeling of oneness?

You arrive at this unity by reconnecting all your divided parts. Through love, you begin to unify. Love unites everything within you, and you return to oneness, wholeness. When you become one, you go back to this eternal life—to the Garden of Eden, to the Kingdom of Heaven. You begin to live the eternal life you were born into as your spirit and body entered the world.

Mother Nature

All beings are part of one life. Regardless of who you are, where you come from, your species, and your actions, you are a part of life. All creatures come together as one.

Imagine it's a beautiful day. It feels like spring. The birds are chirping; it's sunny and warm, with a gentle breeze blowing. You're experiencing the magnificence of the level of life. Unlike the other three levels of body, mind, and love, this one is peaceful, tranquil, aware, and awake. It seems to contain everything—feeling, thinking, and emotions.

This space is so big and feels so safe. It's like a mother looking after three children—the levels of body, mind, and love—and those three are well-behaved without fighting, pulling on each other, or killing each other.

As you practice self-discovery, you'll reach this place. You may want to stay there for half a day. Sometimes you may even wake up in it. It's different to the other three. The other three need to make themselves known; they play up their feelings and actions, and their brain runs non-stop.

Whereas in this level of life, everything is steeped in peace and ease. At the same time, you're quite aware of everything. You're orchestrating everything to work together smoothly, in harmony.

Nothing seems to bother this. Tasks or events that once seemed prominent or insurmountable become small and easy. You can now carry on all your life's duties without hindrance. Stop and start don't exist. Everything is on a continuum. Thoughts and feelings don't stop and start. Actions don't stop and start. Everything flows. Nothing is separate. Division disappears. It's peaceful. The union of love and life is nearly indescribable.

Full of Life

You can only be conscious when you're ready to let go of your dreams. You are love when you're ready to break away from the attachment of love. You're only ready to live when you no longer fear death. Without these things, you won't access or enjoy consciousness.

When we were children, we were full of life. And why is that? Because our bodies, minds, and emotions had not yet developed. We were full of life but didn't know it.

As we age, we develop our bodies, minds, and emotions, diminishing the life within us. As those levels and their development take over, we feel less alive. To change this—to go back to being full of life—you must release attachments to those three levels and open your hearts to living. You must recognise and reduce focus on other levels and make more space for being alive.

Joy, Ecstasy, and Bliss

When you let go of attachment to your body, you experience joy. When you let go of attachment to your mind, you experience ecstasy. When you let go of attachment to love, you experience bliss. It is beautiful.

There's a difference between joy, ecstasy, and bliss.

Joy arises when you encounter something wonderful related to your body and haven't done anything to achieve it. You just feel the joy of whatever it is or are in the moment with it. A little smile comes, and it's delightful.

Ecstasy is of the mind. It is an intense feeling—a feeling of not being present, of having entered a different plane. It, too, is beautiful but is not generated by the body. It's almost as if you feel lost yet remain at ease. You're no longer aware of your surroundings.

And then there is bliss. Bliss has a feeling of presence. It is of the heart of the love. It's the constant opening and closing of the heart. It can be felt in the body, and the mind is quiet. You feel the expansion, a totality. This state is even more beautiful than joy or ecstasy.

It has a feeling of coolness around your body and extremities. It's as if your mind is cool and your body's cooler. You are present, and everything is flowing. Everything is wherever it needs to be. Nothing is misplaced. All is perfect. All is well. Bliss is close to perfection, and it is a beautiful blessing.

Connecting with Life

It isn't easy to reach the energy level of life, even though it seems it would be simple. Most of the time, we are focused on our bodies and our health, in our mind thinking about things, or basking in or grappling with our emotions. We're so involved in these three aspects of being that we don't actually live life.

But once you become content with your body, calm in your mind, and moderate your emotions, you can open yourself to the life right in front of you. Life happens all around us, and often we're never in it. We think we are living life, yet our focus is on our bodies, our thoughts, and our emotions.

Connecting with life is simple. We don't have to travel, climb mountains, sail the seas. None of those things are required for life. Life is right next to you and happening around you every day. Every second. All you have to do is sit and breathe.

Open your body, mind, and heart to connecting with the energy outside of yourself and integrating it with the energy within you. The first step is to be aware of your breathing. Slow down, be, and breathe. Then allow life to happen. Clearly, nothing fancy is required. In fact, life requires embracing simplicity. Holding still, breathing, and being leads to the blessing of life.

Living Life

So what does it mean to live your life? It takes observation and patience to begin living life. When you're still discovering how to be in your body, make the highest use of your mind, and love unconditionally, you're in a phase of growing and developing. You're trying to understand the world. At some level, the discovery process happens in the background without your awareness. Yet, opening your awareness and moving through each day diligently helps you speed up self-discovery.

If you choose to embrace self-discovery, you will eventually attain the level of life. Living arises when you know who you are. Sometimes this process is cyclical. You are connected with body, mind, and love, then shift into living life, and something happens. You fall out of sync and return to focusing on one of the other levels. This cycle is completely human. Pick yourself up and begin again. Suffering and pain happen to all of us and can cause setbacks. Honour that, then move forward again.

Perhaps you have an illness that takes you out of that sublime feeling of life and redirects your focus to your body. Perhaps you experience some sort of heightened level of stress that causes you to focus on your mind. Or maybe you encounter an emotional setback like losing a loved one. Any of these challenges pull you out of that energetic level of a peaceful life. Yet you know what life feels like and how to get there. Pick yourself up and move forward again. You have the most important ingredients to living a beautiful life within you.

You don't need to go off anywhere. You don't need to chase after love, the perfect job, or someone else's idea of perfect health. You are a complete package. Live your life, and continue discovering, breathing, and feeling every moment. This approach to life is subtle and simple. Live with awareness and openness every second of every day. Be satisfied with and cherish whatever is going on around you. Here you will find peace. You're not running after anything. You're not searching for anything. You have found what you're looking for, and it is all inside of you.

Joy comes with peace. You no longer judge whether something is better or worse, beautiful or not beautiful, or good or bad. With this peace and joy comes silence. It's as if everything you've learned on your self-discovery journey so far falls into place. All the pieces fit just where they're meant to. You live as a complete person, an integrated human being.

Eternal Life

You are born into eternal life without even knowing it. Without conscious awareness, you played happily in this eternal space. As you started to grow, you began separating from this eternal life. You learned from family, friends, and school to label things right and wrong, good and bad, and male and female. This separation led to worry, pain, and loss.

These discordant feelings arose because you began dividing yourself into many parts, trying to please or appease those outside yourself. This pain continues until you begin the journey of self-discovery. Until you start looking to become one with yourself again. Until you find that oneness you were born with, that connection to eternal life, eternal peace.

You search. You discover. You grow. You become open and eventually unify, bringing together everything that had once separated. At that moment, you become one again. And when you become one again, you will see who you truly are, how everything was created, and how to live again in eternal life.

The Meaning of Life

Death does not make sense in life because life is aliveness, and there is no space for death. Similarly, separation from God doesn't make any sense because everything within you and outside of you is God. Self-identity comes and goes, yet you're always with God—even if you don't always feel it. All of us originate in the heart of God. It's as simple as that.

So, what is life? It seems very simple. But life is at a higher level when compared to the body, the mind, and love. And we are born into life, yet we grow up and experience separation.

Societal norms cause us to delude ourselves, and we get carried away with the other aspects of living. We try to alter our bodies. We try to learn more. We chase after love. We are not living life because we're too busy trying to attain something else.

Living life means waking up in the morning and simply being. But we've been brought up to focus on body, mind, and love. Our continued focus on those three realms has crowded out our ability to live. For example, we spend so much time thinking that we believe we're living, but in reality, we're only thinking. Or we get so caught up in the rush of emotions that we believe what we're experiencing is life when it is actually just one aspect of living.

Self-discovery helps you curtail and moderate excess in those three areas. You continue to grow but no longer strive for a perfect body, a brilliant mind, and consuming love. You'll begin to live life healthily in an intelligent way. Embracing the innate intelligence of the body, mind, and love helps you begin to maximize life. You are not your body, your mind, your emotions. As a human, you live in these energies.

Consider these aspects of life as separate rooms in a house you own. You enter these rooms, explore them, learn how to maintain them, and exist in them. You move in and out and between them. These rooms represent your energetic layers. You have many energy layers, and these three—body, mind, and love—are the ones you're most familiar with. They're comfortable. You get to know them well and have a healthy relationship with them. But more awaits you. Life is the next level.

The Energy of Life

Life helps you expand beyond the walls of your houses. The energy of life has various names—prana, chi, lifeforce energy, spirit, and many more. It's everywhere. It's all around you. You breathe it in and breathe it out. Whenever you practice yoga, qigong, Reiki, sing, or dance, the lifeforce energy enters you and opens your heart. Lifeforce energy lives in your metaphysical heart. When your heart opens and closes, lifeforce energy goes in and out. When you're stuck in one of the other energy layers, you're unaware of the lifeforce energy.

Most of the time, no one teaches you how to access this lifeforce energy. You must look for it. Yet it is naturally there with you, in the background, like breathing. When you connect with lifeforce energy, living takes on a new tone. You will recognise it in the trees. You'll recognise it in the mountains. You'll recognise it in the sun's rays.

When connected to lifeforce energy, you will appreciate rain and wind. You'll feel compelled to sit outside and observe nature. You'll go for walks. You'll play with animals. You'll see beauty everywhere around you. That's when you know you're living life.

It has nothing to do with anything. It does not care how much money you have in your bank account. It does not care about the shape of your body. It does not care what you've achieved. It does not care who you love.

Life is individual for everybody. It's not dependent. You'll know when you're living because you feel connected to everything. You see the simple beauty, truth, and energy in everything. Living life is very precious.

You're born into life. After self-discovery and reconnecting with life, you return to where you were born. In the energy of life, you feel relaxed, relieved, and free. Your breathing comes easily and fully. You're aware of your heart, and you're aware of everything that is happening around you. You're grounded and stable, and nothing disturbs you. This layer of existence is beautiful, and recognising it is crucial. You've moved away from focusing solely on your bodily needs, rumination, and emotional attachments. You've opened your heart and connected with lifeforce energy.

Beyond Life

Life is beautiful. It is everywhere. Lifeforce energy connects you with the euphoria you were born into. And yet . . . you have more to discover. Beyond this beautiful life is a recognition of your pure potential.

As we continue our journey of self-discovery, this beautiful life is just one stop. As you grow, you'll begin to detach and say goodbye. You'll begin to let go of whatever life has brought you—your work, family, love, and everything else. Yet this releasing is peaceful. You no longer obsess over or want things. You'll happily use or interact with whatever comes your way, but rather than chasing or demanding, you'll let things flow to you.

Letting go of the constructs of life leads to freedom, to living forever.

Awakening

Imagine starting your day in a new and different way—awakening! It's as though you're out of your body seeing yourself standing on planet Earth. You're no longer an individual. You've expanded and can see all the other human beings.

You see the Earth, which gives form to all beings and nourishes all. You see that everyone is caught up in the unconscious ocean soup as big as the continents, and it provides energy for all creation on the planet. You see that all are caught in this unconsciousness and are working for this planet to keep it moving and growing. You're wide awake and aware, but others are asleep.

Now, imagine recognizing how overwhelming it is to be human—to be you. The chaos of everything you're involved with, your surroundings, and your relationships keeps you occupied in this unconsciousness further. The many forces acting on the earth can keep you asleep for a long time, and hence becoming awake can be very difficult. You've replaced that glorious cosmic consciousness with drab and dreary unconsciousness.

Your awareness is an ideal tool to enhance, expand your consciousness and awaken to the glory of the cosmos.

Moving Toward Light

You have a choice. As you practice self-discovery, you'll have access to that cosmic perspective of inter-connectedness more often and more clearly. Trust and know it is available to you. Practice remaining open, awake, and aware. When you're at that level of life, you're ready to move into light.

Chapter 10:

Level 5: Light

Your journey of self-discovery moves you toward light. As you expand your journey into discovering who you are, you begin to detach from other aspects of life. Awareness of self and openness to self during this process of discovering who you are is not an act of selfishness. It is an act of love, of spirit.

You grow so you can become a better person and be of service. You might occasionally wonder, "If I devote myself to self-discovery, won't I be disregarding other essential aspects of being human? Should I spend this much time on meditating or working on personal growth"? A feeling of conflict is normal.

But remember, you are shifting into a different way of living. You are expanding. You're here and now and more present than ever, savouring each moment.

What Is Light?

When you've mastered the level of life, you begin to open to light. Sometimes you see the light through love. Early in the self-discovery journey, you're aware of your heart. It's present, but you don't notice it. However, once you enter the level of life energy, you become more acutely aware of your heart—like it is almost breathing. Eventually, you become aware of it all the time, and that's when you shift out of life and connect with light.

Though we all have a connection with love, certain people have a radiant energy of love sourced from a higher level. You feel a sense of longing, a deep warmth, a subtle pull, a contentment in their presence—whether they're physically with you, afar, or have passed away. When encountering someone whose love comes from light, it's almost like you can feel it on the right side of your chest.

When this pull of love on the right of your chest dissolves, you become aware of the left side of your chest. Life is connected to the left chest; it's your place of aliveness. You want to walk with your friend. You want to have a delicious meal with your family. You can create that. You've discovered your strength and know your body, mind, and love express themselves perfectly in your life. You are with others, and yet you're with light.

The light now oversees your heart, though it's very difficult to pinpoint where this light is coming from at first. Perhaps you feel it in front of your forehead, but as your self-discovery progresses and you continue to do Power Flow Practice, you see that the light is originating from the core. You will see this light as the sun. It shines over your life which lives in your heart. The sun and your heart—light, and life—are coordinated, existing in harmony. As the light shines over your heart and the life within the heart, you're content, joyful, cheerful, and rejuvenated because light enhances life.

The light radiating from the core of you is exactly like the sun shining over life on Earth. It's as simple as that. The light shining over you is the light shining through the universe. You can use this light to heal yourself, or you can transmit this light to heal other people.

When you give up thinking about external factors and open your attention to self-discovery, you're connecting with light. When you give up the love of everything else in life and focus on just loving yourself as you are, you're connecting with light.

You do not sacrifice the mundane for the sake of the sacred. You balance them both. You're harmonious, revelling in euphoria.

Light as Spirituality

Light is the energy of the sun and the energy of the lifeforce. The most effective method for discovering who you are and connecting with light is through Power Flow Practice.

Clear your mind. Empty it of thoughts. Follow the light. Through this journey, you will encounter many hurdles. Clearing your body is the first step, followed by clearing your mind, followed by clearing your heart. Eventually, you'll arrive at the light.

God—or whatever term you use for Universal Energy—is the supreme light and is completely unique. The relationship connection between God and humans is love. When you attain the level of life, you're blissful. You begin to see your connection with God, the life-giver.

A triangle relationship begins. Humans anchor one corner. Love anchors another corner. Light, or God, anchors the third. When the corners are connected and in balance, euphoria bubbles up.

Spirituality in itself isn't anything. Spirituality is a tool. It's a tool, a torch, a flame, or an awareness that shines light on who we are. Its purpose is to help us discover ourselves. Learning how to use the tool is the essence of spirituality. Through its use, you begin to see yourself. You begin to see who you are and discover your highest self. It helps you move from level to level. Spirituality is about discovering your energies and connecting with the deepest part of yourself.

All of us are within God, and God is within all of us; we just don't always know it. To connect with God, live from your heart and open yourself to the light. We're often lost in our problems, worries, and suffering, and we don't remember to connect with spirit. We forget we live in the heart of God and that God is in our hearts. We can't see or touch God, so it becomes easy to forget.

Living in Harmony

Why do you need to discover the light? What is the benefit of being spiritual? Spiritual development and connection to the light are tools to aid us in our self-discovery journey. Discovering who you are leads to peace. Follow the light. Follow spirituality. Practice it; discover it. Light frees you from attachments and leads to liberation. It is the gateway to freedom.

Imagine waking with awareness. The sun shines outside, and its brightness symbolizes light. The sun represents the spiritually supported active state of mind. You're effortlessly productive. You're outward facing and active. Yet you feel at ease in all you do.

The day passes, and you watch the sunset and the moon rise. With the light of the moon, you begin to slow down and turn inward. You feel a deeper sense of relaxation and calm, almost like meditation.

The sun and moon—day and night—balance each other. They are in harmony. The sun leads in the daytime, and the moon leads at night. Attune yourself to this harmony as you grow, expand, and discover who you are.

Moving Toward Energy Synthesis

As you find and live in that balance between life and light, you're evolving. You're becoming the person you were born to be. Yet, more still awaits you. It's time to move to the next level, energy synthesis.

Chapter 11:

Level 6: Energy Synthesis

Energy synthesis combines all the energy layers within you. The layers you move through every single day in life. These energies are divided; they're not whole. Each energy layer is different from the other. The energies of the body, mind, love, life, and light are unique and separate. They have their own laws and rules and work in accordance with those laws.

Every human follows the same energy rules. Each does what is required to keep the energy flowing across the layers. Since the energy layers are divided, it is up to you to bring them together. You do this through cultivating spirituality and working with light.

As you discover who you are, you more clearly recognise each and every energy level. You go into them and come out of them. You learn about them, understand them, and master them. Then you let them go.

Sometimes it is easy to get stuck in a particular energy level. Perhaps you function well at a particular level. It is comfortable so you stay there for a while. But to grow— to move toward liberation—you must choose to deeply understand each energy level but be willing to detach and grow when the time is right. By uniting all the energies, you move into energy synthesis.

What is Energy Synthesis?

Each energy layer has strengths and weaknesses. Within each energy level is a duality that makes us feel high or low. Balancing these energies daily helps us overcome overwhelm. You may become excited when you enter a new energy level for the first time. You feel exhilaration, but once that feeling of newness wears off, you may feel downcast.

To balance this surge of energy and avoid being carried away by it, you must continue cultivating self-awareness. This self-awareness, combined with self-discovery, helps you navigate energy synthesis. You notice and feel all the energies coming together, circulating, rejuvenating, and becoming one. They're becoming pure. They're creating a new you. You're existing in a new system.

In this new system, you attain a new body, new mind, new love, new life, and a new light. This new you exists in energy synthesis. You've learned from and mastered the other energy levels, and now you're more than you ever were before.

You have to come to a point where you are aware of all the different layers of energies that exist within you and outside of you. You've recognised and mastered them. You know when you're focused on your body or your thoughts. You know when you're feeling love. You know the euphoria of life and light. You know each level has its purpose, its reason for being. You've learned what you need to about each, and now you've attained an ability to balance all energy levels comfortably. You feel awe but not overwhelm.

Moving Toward Being

Once you're comfortable existing in energy synthesis, you can move upward again. You no longer need to learn from individual levels anymore. You detach from them and live in a place of energy synthesis. All the energy within you is purified, and you're ready to move on. From this foundation of energy synthesis, you move into the next step. You move into a space of pure being.

Part 3:

Transformation

Chapter 12:

Being

The following questions often arise on the journey of discovering who you are, "Who am I? What am I"? Even without the self-discovery process, people often ask themselves this question. And that is where the final level—transitioning to being—comes into play. At that level, you discover who you are.

Attaining the level of being is about bringing together your multiple millions of sensations, thoughts, and feelings—the elements you identify with daily. When all those disparate aspects dissolve into one, you begin to see who you are. This one awareness is the observer of your life, the silent witness not created by nature and earth.

This being, which you call "self", does not reside in the energy realm. But as you deepen your awareness and shift from life to light to energy synthesis, you become formless. This formlessness is no longer identified with anything. The formlessness gives rise to all thought and all beings and all life.

Who Is a Being?

As a being, you are a transparent witness and observer. You integrate and flow through all the energy levels you've mastered. You've moved up the energy pyramid and attained the level of energy synthesis. From that point, you cross over a border to the other side and become a new being.

You witness everything wholly without needing to understand minute details. You no longer try to observe or learn. You just are. It's like looking through a window. Your being is on one side, and on the other side are all the different layers. You view those layers without purpose. You're not looking specifically at or for anything. You simply see and are at peace.

This is a beautiful way of existing. At first, it may be unfamiliar and uncomfortable to be without thought and emotion. Yet it's okay. Trust the sensation. Be open to harmonizing with what is without reservations.

It's freeing to breathe from the depth of your soul. You can let go of all your tightness and grasping. You used to try to control everything, making things happen or preventing them. Yet now, in this state of being, you can fully relax. Every cell of your body, your mind, and your heart is wide open.

Being is a natural state. You no longer pass judgement—making things bigger or smaller, or good or bad. Everything simply happens. Flow. Feel the freedom and opening of your heart. Bask in the beauty.

When you are in the state of being, you reflect all the energies you interact with. When interacting with your body's energy, your being is aware of and supportive of your body. Your being offers wisdom and healing to the energies of the body.

When connected to the state of being, you become more deeply aware of the other energy levels and interact with them from a place of higher consciousness and insight. Attaining a connection to the level of being leads you to a profound awareness of your life.

You've moved beyond wandering lost in the energies of your body, mind, heart, love, and light. You're fully conscious. You're in harmony. You see all that you need to see. You no longer manipulate the world, nor are manipulated by it. This state of being is whole and separates you from the grasping nature of individual energy levels.

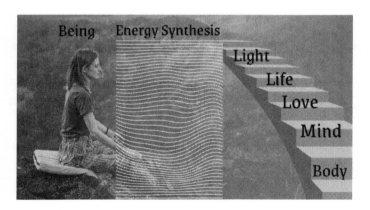

You, and all living things, are connected to this state from the moment of birth. You don't need to create it. You simply need to re-discover it and then bask in awareness of it.

Being as the Ocean

Imagine the state of being an ocean. You've lived a life of thought. Some thoughts are simple, and others complex. Some thoughts are ugly, and others beautiful. In your lifetime, you've had millions of thoughts. Thoughts are what you know, what you're comfortable with.

Now you've arrived at this state of being. It stretches in front of you like a vast sea. You're worried that you—and your millions of thoughts—will dissolve into this huge ocean. You're worried you'll no longer be an individual. You fear that the ocean is separate from you.

Yet, have faith. The ocean is beautiful. It is made of love, intelligence, and compassion. Do not be frightened or fearful. You're an amazingly beautiful human to have come this far. You're creative and whole and will survive.

The ocean is infinite love. You can be yourself while harmonizing with everything else. You can work as one, and you can work as part of the whole.

Listen to the ocean. It says, "I love you. I see you. We will always be together. We can work as one. You love me. Do not worry. Relax into me and become me. I'll take care of you. Be at peace".

Entering the state of being means completely letting go of your body, mind, heart, and life as you know it. It is a state of joy, bliss, and ecstasy together. You have become that. You are that. In every moment of every day, you're whole.

Being and Healing

We all are born as healers. Each of us excels at healing ourselves and others on specific energy levels. One person is skilled in healing the body. Another is adept at healing emotions or love. Some could be proficient at healing in the energy of life, while others are well-skilled at healing in the energy of light.

Intuitively, almost unconsciously, you use this gift to heal yourself. It comes quite easily to you. You likely wouldn't even consider calling yourself a healer at this point, yet you unconsciously help others simply by being yourself.

Every day—at work, at home, during conversations, at the gym, with your children, with your parents—you offer healing, and you don't even know it. In every action and every relationship, you transmit healing energy. You don't have to be qualified or trained. Being you is enough. Healing is a natural part of life.

So in this way, healers help other healers. Interacting with others allows you a chance to help heal others and the chance to receive healing for yourself.

On this self-discovery journey, you learn about various energy layers. You become an expert in your current layer while learning about other layers. You then ascend until you reach this point of becoming a new being. From here, you innately yet consciously help others—for the pleasure of it, for the joy of it, and because it is what you are born to do. As this new being, you are serving your highest purpose.

New Being Meditation

This meditation helps you practice detachment so you can step off the emotional roller coaster you encounter while moving through energy levels.

Attachment is a form of self-protection. Through life, you've learned how to work with body, mind, and love. You're familiar with these levels. They're comfortable. But allow yourself to step out of your comfort zone and grow into expansion.

Find a comfortable place to sit or lie down. Close your eyes and breathe deeply and fully. Allow your heart to empty. Pluck the emotions from your heart, and pour them out. Empty your heart of the impurities that have filled it through life. All the pain, anger, and heartbreak.

Once your heart is empty, fill that space with unconditional love, compassion, and limitless abundance. Your body still exists, but you have an unlimited sense of expansion.

This is your new now, and things simply happen. You do not think or force anything to happen. You're in the realm of pure God-sourced action.

Offer this unconditional love to all the people you touch and have relationships with. Expand that unconditional love out broadly like stars in the universe. From that expanded state, you begin to feel a pulsation and pull on the right side of your heart.

You acknowledge it and honour it, then are drawn to the centre of your heart. From this space, you notice something in front of you. It is the essence of a giant person wearing a glowing white robe. You feel tiny yet safe.

You stand before this immense white-robed essence and feel a connection to God. In this presence, all the pain in your heart is dissolved. You feel almost as if you've been given a new, open, and expansive heart.

With your new heart and with the comfort and confidence bestowed upon you by the essence in the glowing robe, you find yourself drawn into a long dark purple tunnel. It is cosy and warm and hidden.

Then, while in that tunnel, you begin to notice a warm golden light. This golden glow expands and becomes you. You're golden inside and outside your body.

This glowing warmth is familiar. As you bask in it, you realise that you always had this warm golden glow within you. It is the essence of you.

The person you've always been, your consistent self, has expanded. Your heart is pure, and you've become radiating golden energy. You're form and formlessness at the same time. All aspects of you emit this warm golden light. Every cell, every part of you, is filled with this.

You recognise yourself as you—the body, mind, and emotions you've always lived with—but now you know you're something bigger. Something pure, open, expansive, and connected to the cosmos.

Your mind is empty. Your heart is empty. You are filled with light. You've unified all your energies.

Your discipline and hard work of discovering who you are helped you let go of all your desires and attachments and move through all your energy layers to reach a level of energy synthesis.

You enter your beautiful life in a way that connects all your energy from the lowest to the highest. You have arrived. You are liberated. You are a new being. You are unlimited potential.

Chapter 13:

Liberation

When you reach a place of liberation, nothing is left to learn of yourself. All the learning, all the searching, all the knowing, all the understanding, all the thinking, all the analysing is finished. You no longer need to strive, grasp, grow, or evolve. You are completely free.

You have reached a state of liberation of the body, liberation of the mind, liberation of love, liberation in life, liberation of light, and liberation of all combined energies. Transcending all these levels is what leads to your final liberation. You have discovered who you are. You know and honour your unlimited potential. You are new.

Reaching Liberation

You experience liberation when you've recognised all the different layers of energies that operate within you and outside of you, and you've mastered them. You're not attached to them anymore. You're not pulled back into reliving those layers again.

Once you've done that, you've purified yourself and entered the point of energy synthesis where everything is completely cleared and rejuvenated. You move across to the other side and shift into a state of pure being or pure consciousness. You are no longer attached to the other energy layers. The next step beyond the being is liberation.

Sometimes it is difficult to recognise this pure state of being. It's like when your plate is filled with food. You can't see the plate, yet it carries the food on top of it. So once you clear the food—the various energy levels—you are left with the plate. Without the plate, it would have been harder, perhaps impossible, to enjoy the food—enjoy all the beautiful energies you had before.

So the plate is pretty much like you—the new being, naked and pure, without any trace of life's energies present. When you now let go of the plate, the new being, it leads to total liberation.

As you ease into the being, you recognise a feeling that has been with you since birth. It has always been there. Yet as you grew up, the forces of life tainted, manipulated, and played around with your energies. You could never relax into yourself because mundane energies absorbed your attention. But once these energies clear and you pass the point of energy synthesis, you see yourself completely. You see who you are.

This emptiness of mundane energies highlights the presence of your true self—your true being. This being is so beautiful that you wish to sit with it all day long. After experiencing this true self for quite a while, when you've experienced being the empty plate or the empty vessel, you realise you have one more step to take.

You no longer need to be an empty vessel. You let go of the being—the vessel. You move beyond the gap. You move into liberation, into freedom. It's nearly unexplainable. It is exquisite. This liberation—this freedom—unfetters you from everything.

Tranquillity

The feeling of liberation is like being in a place of suspension, of space. You feel continuous, calm, tranquil, peaceful, harmonious, loving, expansive, clear, awake, and endless.

Nothing is separate; all is whole. You're not pulled to do anything. You're not pushed to do anything. You don't look for anything. You don't need anything. You're barely hungry. You're barely thinking. You feel no emotions.

It's a monotone existence, all on one plane. There's no separation or division. Your mind is free, calm, and at peace. Emotion is at rest. Your body is relaxed. Nothing needs to be done. You don't even know what you're meant to do in this space because you're not drawn to action. You're content in stillness. Whether you do something or not, nothing will change the space. You're surrounded by it, and it is within you.

This space of liberation and emptiness also gives you access to creation. You can speak, act, and create new ideas and new forms. You're in the flow. Things created in this liberated space begin to take on a life of their own. They're energised differently than things created in the mundane world.

Unconsciousness versus Emptiness

What is the difference between unconsciousness and emptiness? Unconsciousness is when you don't know who you are. When you're lost in yourself, yet you think you know yourself. Whatever you see, whatever is around you isn't quite real.

You haven't discovered who you are. You live in a state of confusion. You're lost. You're dragged to wherever life pulls you. You're reactive rather than creative, living in a state of numbness. You're not awake. You're not aware. You're not in control of your life. You're floating.

Yet, there is tremendous love in unconsciousness. You feel exuberance and connectedness, which is a beautiful thing. You are fulfilled in this unconsciousness where you have tremendous love around you, and you're lost in this love, but you don't know who you are.

Eventually, you come to a point where you want to discover who you are. When you're tired of floating, drifting, being lost, dreamy, and unproductive, you wake up. You start to distance yourself from the mundane daily things that contribute to unconsciousness. You slowly, step by step, back up and observe yourself. Bit by bit, you'll broaden your awareness. Then you come to who you are. Discover who you are.

And when you discover who you are—finally being and living who you are meant to be—you shift. You experience your real self. You are fulfilled by who you are. Then it's time to let go. You let go of the past. You let go of the mundane and material world and move into light. You move into your true being and cross the gap into liberation. You experience spaciousness, emptiness, and vacancy. Nothing is left. There used to be something you thought was you, but that is gone—at least for a moment.

This is the difference between being unconscious and being empty. Emptiness comes when you completely let go of your accumulation of energies.

The Gap

This space of liberation and emptiness is silent. Its quality of love is different from ordinary human love. Most of the time, what we think is love is actually an emotion. But in this liberated space, love is a conscious awakening.

When you are aware of everything that is happening, and it's one continuous moment, you experience expansion. It's a sense of peace, and everything flows. You're not thinking or doing. Everything simply happens.

You notice that when you meet, connect with, or speak with others, you bring them into this space with you. You invite them in so they can experience it even though they are not yet ready to live there.

Existing in this place of liberation sometimes makes you feel out of breath. Like you need something to attach yourself to. That is the opposite feeling of being in this space. You are still human and need to live in the world. Perhaps this space of liberation is not yet permanent, and that's okay. You're expected to slip and have your body, mind, and emotions act up. Your humanity pulls you out of this space.

It's almost like you can see a physical gap between this space of liberation and everyday life. You notice the gap most when you begin to feel pulled back into mundane life. You see the gap. You sense it.

You love being in the space of liberation, but that feeling of breathlessness urges you to shift. You feel pushed to do something, to achieve something. You feel compelled to watch TV or go to work or meet a friend or listen to music. You know that life is waiting for you beyond the gap.

And, truthfully, doing mundane stuff is fun. Living an ordinary human life is fun, yet it is less peaceful than this place of liberation.

So essentially, you have two ways of existing—in the ordinary realm of humanity and in the transcendent space of liberation.

Moving Toward Unlimited Potential

What is beyond liberation? How could anything be better than that space of openness, oneness, and connectedness? You have one more realm left to explore, the realm of unlimited potential.

Chapter 14:

Unlimited Potential

When you reach a point of unlimited potential, you write a new story for everything in life. You are the creator of your life. In actuality, you are starting from scratch. You are intelligent, open, clever, bright, aware, awake, loving, kind, compassionate, and caring.

With all you've uncovered so far on this discovery of yourself and all you've accomplished to this point, you are now ready to begin your new life.

You've attained a level of awe-filled beauty. It feels a little unexplainable. Until now, you had ideas. You wanted to achieve something, to get somewhere, to run away, to accomplish, to succeed, to let go, and to detach. The duality of the push and pull you experienced in life helped you reach a point of unlimited potential.

Unlimited potential is the heart of creation. From this state, you have the capacity to write, draw, paint, speak, sing, dance—whatever form of creation resonates with you—the most beautiful, loving, joyful, caring, affectionate, and compassionate existence. It is an existence you'd never yet dreamed possible. You have complete and ultimate freedom—no one is judging you, watching over you, telling you what to do or how to do it, or stopping you. You have a new gift, and with it, you begin a new journey.

You've walked the winding path of discovering who you are. You have learned to empty your body, mind, and heart. You've detached from the constraints of the past. You have floated in an ocean of newness. Now you are liberated, and in this liberation, you become unlimited potential. In this unlimited potential, you get to create anything you wish.

Finding the Fire

At the point of liberation, a fire lights within you. And what is this fire? It is the energy of unlimited potential. It is at the very core of you. At the core of who you are all these years, all these days, all these months, all while you experimented with and learned different forms of energies.

Throughout your journey, you've been playing with and engaging with energies. You identify yourself by thinking, *I am the body and the mind; I am love, life, and light.* You identified your stages of evolution from childhood to adulthood, and you thought you knew who you were. But in truth, as you truly discover who you are, you understand all the different layers and let them go.

You even acknowledge that you are simply an observer of your life.

And then . . . and then you let go.

You step into the gap.

You cross over into liberation.

You connect with your pure potential.

You now have freedom you've never experienced before. A freeness that is unlimited potential.

This fire that has been lit at your core—this fire of unlimited potential—can be used to forge anything you wish. Create anything you like from this point onwards. Now you get to write the story of the life you'd like to live. You're free. You can manifest and have everything you'd like in life. This fire burns forever. Make the most of this life you've been given.

Final Thoughts

Here you are. You have gone through all the different layers of the energies: the body, mind, love, life, and light. You have explored, learned about, and understood different levels of energies. You've practiced and implemented them. You've mastered them. You now recognise them in your everyday life.

You've reached a level of energy synthesis—a union of all the energies that arise after mastering each layer and detaching from each layer. You're no longer carrying anything forward. You've freed yourself from identifying with any one layer. You've attained a connection to pure energy. From this place, body, mind, love, and life are in harmony.

Then you took the next step. You became a new being, an empty being. The being who's just a witness and simply observes without any purpose. That essence of being has been with you since birth, and now you sense it, know it, and live it.

After appreciating this sense of being and its emptiness, you've gone one step further. You're now liberated from the being also.

When you're whole and connected to the universe, you embody everything. You're the house. You're the tree. You're your friends and family. You're the car. You're the bird. You're the cloud. You are everything, and you have everything. You no longer stand in isolation. You've unified yourself within yourself, and now you unify with everything outside of you. You are a material form, and you are subtle energy.

As you discover who you are, as you travel the path, you shift from having everything to losing everything to becoming everything. This is lifetime learning. Perhaps you'll only find liberation the moment before you die.

Continue growing. You'll progress, then have setbacks. Pick yourself up and start again. Don't give up. Take the leap. Put in the effort. Have the discipline.

Discovering who you are is the best gift you can give yourself in this lifetime.

I'd love to work with you through The School of Enlightenment if you want support on your journey. You have two options.

Visit www.theschoolforenlightenment.com to learn about all the programs and courses available.

To learn more about The Levels of Being specifically, visit this website, bit.ly/3Y21sEL, which takes you to the *Discover Who You Are* online course. You can also find that course through this QR code.

Discover Who You Are Workbook

If you enjoyed reading this book,
take your transformation to the next level by using the
Discover Who You Are Workbook.

**Be one of the first 100 people to request the
workbook, and get your copy FREE.**

Receive your free copy by sending an email to:
theschoolforenlightenment@gmail.com.

In the subject line, enter the phrase **Workbook**.

Acknowledgements

I'd like to thank my family, friends, and other spiritual and non-spiritual members of my life who have directly or indirectly contributed to this book and made this journey possible.

About Smitha

Smitha Jagadish has loved the written word since she was a little girl, always using a diary or journal to express herself. She often jokes, "Even though I was raised in India and knew very little English, I've now written two books in English"! She resides in beautiful England with her hubby, two children, and a pet dog.

Smitha Jagadish writes spiritual books about meditation, awakening, wisdom teachings, self-discovery, and how to work with the universe. She is a spiritual teacher who offers training courses that help new seekers navigate the tricky waters of self-discovery. She also offers a training program for spiritual coaches. Learn more at www.theschoolforenlightenment.com.

A Favor to Ask

Thank you for taking the time to read this book.

I hope you have found it thought-provoking
and inspiring.
I'd love to hear your feedback,
so please head on over to Amazon or wherever you
purchased this book to leave an honest review for me.
Every review matters, and your responses help me
make future books better.

I thank you endlessly.

Printed in Great Britain
by Amazon

32489599R00070